F-FREEZING ABC

Posy Simmonds

F-FREEZING ABC

Posy Simmonds

RED FOX

For Raphael

Picture books by Posy Simmonds in Red Fox

FRED
F-FREEZING ABC
BOUNCING BUFFALO

A Red Fox Book

Published by Random House Children's Books
20 Vauxhall Bridge Road, London SW1V 2SA

A division of Random House UK Ltd
London Melbourne Sydney Auckland
Johannesburg and agencies throughout the world

Copyright © Posy Simmonds 1995

1 3 5 7 9 10 8 6 4 2

First published in Great Britain by Jonathan Cape Limited 1995
Red Fox edition 1998

All rights reserved.

Printed in Hong Kong

RANDOM HOUSE UK Limited Reg. No. 954009

ISBN 0 09 955001 6

A-Anteater

"A-A-Atishoo!" sneezed the Anteater.
"I-it's a-absolutely ar-ar-arctic!"

B-Bear   C-Cat

"Brrr!" shivered the Bear.
"It's b-b-bitter!"
"C-cold!" complained the Cat.

D-Duck

"Shut up!" said the Duck.
"Stop moaning! N-next door
have got a n-nice w-warm house...
...L-let's g-go round there."

So they all went to see the
E-Elephant.

"But, of course! Come in!"
cried the Elephant.
"Make yourselves at home!"

"Stop squashing me!" wailed the Cat.
"Oh, let's go somewhere else!"

Across the fields, they found the

F-Fox.

"We're f-f-freezing!" said the Duck.
"*You* can sit by my fire," said
the Fox, licking his chops.
"N-n-no f-fear!" flapped the Duck.

They called out to the
G-Goat.

"You're most welcome,"
said the Goat. "I've got a *huge*
H-House."

But the house was as cold as an ice box
and echoed with ghostly moans...

"Hmm…that was a short visit," grunted the Goat.

"Oooh, it's icy!" shivered the Anteater.
"L-let's go inside th-this

I-Igloo."

But there were insects hibernating in the igloo...

OW!
OW!
OW!

The Anteater jigged down to the **J**-Jetty ...and jumped!

"He can't swim can he?" observed the **K**-Kangaroo.

"No, dumbo, he *can't!*" shrieked the Cat.

Luckily, the L-Lion had a lifebelt...

"Getting dark!" quacked the Duck.
"Why not shelter in the lighthouse,"
suggested the Lion.

Up came the **M**-Moon, on came the **N**-Night.

The waves boomed and crashed.
The Duck panicked:
"Let's get out of here!"

"H-help!" cried the Duck. "We'll freeze to death!"

"Oooo dear!" hooted the O-Owl.

"No problem," said the P-Pig. "We know the perfect place for you..."

"It's just over the hill," called the Q-Quail.

"Here you are," said the

R-Rabbit.

"You'll be as snug as bugs in there!"

Outside, it had begun to
blow a blizzard.

"Here...use this U-Umbrella," said the skunk.

"Let's g-go home!"
shivered the Cat.
"L-let's b-b-borrow this
V-Van."

But they woke up the

W - Wolf...

...who chased them through the woods...

"Help!" panted the Bear.
"Stop the Wolf...he's
after us...!"

"Just you sit and listen to our X-Xylophone!" bellowed the Y-Yak.

The Wolf nipped past the Yak and

Z-Zig-Zagged down the hill.

But he was too late.

"There you are!" cried the Elephant.
"I've made your house
nice and warm!"

"Oof! s'like an oven in here!"
gasped the Bear.
"It's roasting!" mewed the Cat.
"I'm going...to...pass...out,"
moaned the Duck.

"That's more like it!"

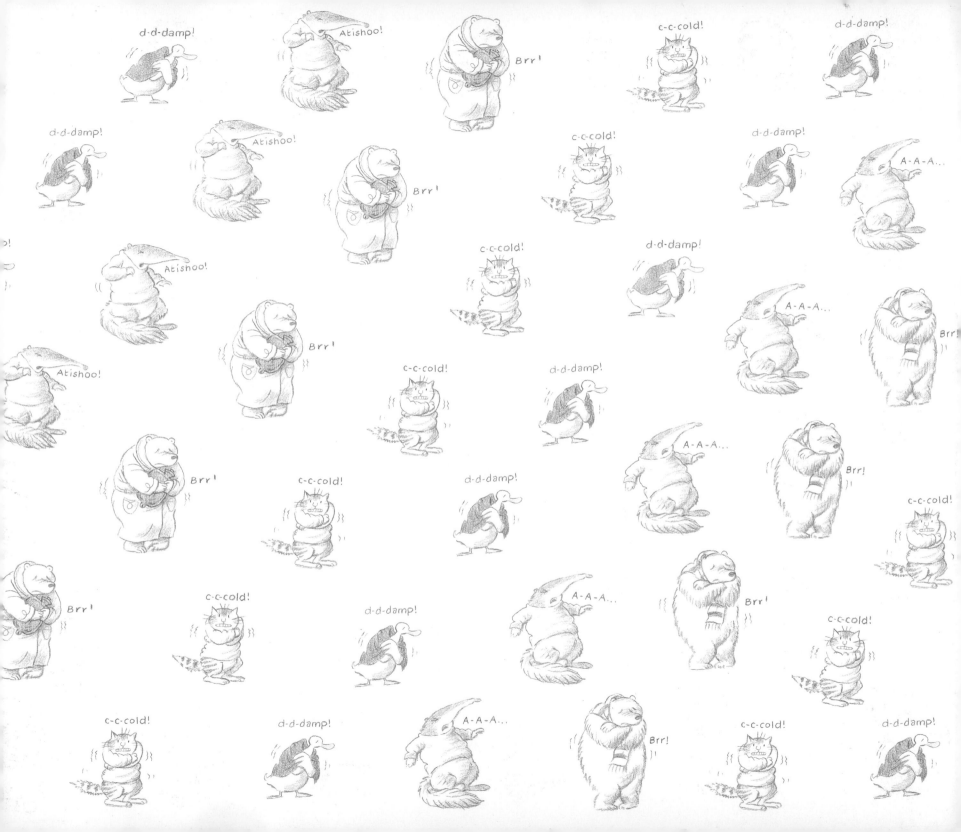

Some bestselling Red Fox picture books

THE BIG ALFIE AND ANNIE ROSE STORYBOOK
by Shirley Hughes
OLD BEAR
by Jane Hissey
OI! GET OFF OUR TRAIN
by John Burningham
I WANT A CAT
by Tony Ross
NOT NOW, BERNARD
by David McKee
ALL JOIN IN
by Quentin Blake
THE SAND HORSE
by Michael Foreman and Ann Turnbull
BAD BORIS GOES TO SCHOOL
by Susie Jenkin-Pearce
BILBO'S LAST SONG
by J.R.R. Tolkien
WILLY AND HUGH
by Anthony Browne
THE WINTER HEDGEHOG
by Ann and Reg Cartwright
A DARK, DARK TALE
by Ruth Brown
HARRY, THE DIRTY DOG
by Gene Zion and Margaret Bloy Graham
DR XARGLE'S BOOK OF EARTHLETS
by Jeanne Willis and Tony Ross
JAKE
by Deborah King